Understanding
God's Purpose
for Your Life

SIGNIFICANCE

Interactions Small Group Series

InterActions
small group series

Understanding
God's Purpose
for Your Life

SIGNIFICANCE

Previously published as *Freedom*

BILL HYBELS

WITH KEVIN AND SHERRY HARNEY

ZONDERVAN™

GRAND RAPIDS, MICHIGAN 49530 USA

WILLOW
Willow Creek Resources

ZONDERVAN™

Significance
Copyright © 1997 by Willow Creek Association
Previously published as *Freedom*

Requests for information should be addressed to:
Zondervan, *Grand Rapids, Michigan 49530*

ISBN-10: 0-310-26603-3
ISBN-13: 0-310-26603-7

Interior design by Rick Devon and Michelle Espinoza

Printed in the United States of America

05 06 07 08 09 10 11 12 /❖ DCI/ 10 9 8 7 6 5 4 3 2 1

CONTENTS

INTERACTIONS

In 1992, Willow Creek Community Church, in partnership with Zondervan and the Willow Creek Association, released a curriculum for small groups entitled the Walking with God series. In just three years, almost a half million copies of these small group study guides were being used in churches around the world. The phenomenal response to this curriculum affirmed the need for relevant and biblical small group materials.

At the writing of this curriculum, there are nearly 3,000 small groups meeting regularly within the structure of Willow Creek Community Church. We believe this number will increase as we continue to place a central value on small groups. Many other churches throughout the world are growing in their commitment to small group ministries as well, so the need for resources is increasing.

In response to this great need, the Interactions small group series has been developed. Willow Creek Association and Zondervan have joined together to create a whole new approach to small group materials. These discussion guides are meant to challenge group members to a deeper level of sharing, to create lines of accountability, to move followers of Christ into action, and to help group members become fully devoted followers of Christ.

SUGGESTIONS FOR INDIVIDUAL STUDY

1. Begin each session with prayer. Ask God to help you understand the passage and to apply it to your life.
2. A good modern translation, such as the New International Version, the New American Standard Bible, or the New Revised Standard Version, will give you the most help. Questions in this guide are based on the New International Version.
3. Read and reread the passage(s). You must know what the passage says before you can understand what it means and how it applies to you.
4. Write your answers in the spaces provided in the study guide. This will help you to express clearly your understanding of the passage.
5. Keep a Bible dictionary handy. Use it to look up unfamiliar words, names, or places.

Suggestions for Group Study

1. Come to the session prepared. Careful preparation will greatly enrich your time in group discussion.
2. Be willing to join in the discussion. The leader of the group will not be lecturing, but will encourage people to discuss what they have learned in the passage. Plan to share what God has taught you in your individual study.
3. Stick to the passage being studied. Base your answers on the verses being discussed rather than on outside authorities such as commentaries or your favorite author or speaker.
4. Try to be sensitive to the other members of the group. Listen attentively when they speak, and be affirming whenever you can. This will encourage more hesitant members of the group to participate.
5. Be careful not to dominate the discussion. By all means participate, but allow others to have equal time.
6. If you are the discussion leader, you will find additional suggestions and helpful ideas in the Leader's Notes.

Additional Resources and Teaching Materials

At the end of this study guide you will find a collection of resources and teaching materials to help you in your growth as a follower of Christ. You will also find resources that will help your church develop and build fully devoted followers of Christ.

Introduction: Understanding God's Purpose for Your Life

Early in my adult ministry I went out to lunch with a friend who said to me, "You have been working with young people over the past years, haven't you?" I said, "Yes, mainly high school students." He continued, "Well, do you have a surprise in store for you!"

My friend had a few things to tell me. He said, "Do you know what you are going to find? Kids and young people are still flexible and willing to change. Transformation is pretty easy for them. But adults resist change at all cost."

Talk about someone dashing the dreams of an idealistic young pastor! I thought to myself, *I hope he is wrong.* I had every intention of praying and preaching my heart out to the adults who would come to this new church. I had hopes of massive, dramatic, cloud-parting transformation happening in the lives of every one of them.

Do you know what I found out over the years? That my well-intentioned friend was wrong—dead wrong. I have discovered that most adults do change . . . for the worst! This is no exaggeration. I really believe it.

Show me a thirty-year-old who wants to lose five pounds, and I will show you the same person fifteen years later who needs to lose twenty pounds. Show me an eighteen-year-old homosexual who feels guilty over having three immoral encounters a year, and I will show you the same person ten years later who is looking for three thrills a week. Show me someone who worries too much at seventeen, and I'll show you the same person at forty who has ulcers and high blood pressure. You see the point. Adults are often on a gradual slide from bad to worse.

Our bodies are in the process of slow deterioration. Sadly, our behavior patterns also have a way of deteriorating over time. Instead of improving, our problems and bad habits become increasingy more serious. After years of unsuccessful attempts at trying to change these patterns, we find ourselves wearing out, giving up, giving in. We feel enslaved to the chains that seem to keep us from moving forward. We wonder if there is any hope of freedom, any meaning beyond the strugle.

I have great news for you today. God not only gives the hope of freedom, He promises much more! In this series of interactions we will discover how to break the chains that hold us and how to discover the significance and purpose we have always hungered to experience. The apostle Paul wrote, "It is for freedom that Christ has set us free. Stand firm, then, and do not let yourselves be burdened again by a yoke of slavery" (Gal. 5:1).

My prayer is for you to experience God's significance and purpose to the fullest and to watch as He breaks the chains that bind you.

Bill Hybels

GOD'S PASSIONATE LOVE

THE BIG PICTURE

I received a phone call late one night from a man who asked me to meet him at a local restaurant. As I drove over, I knew something was very wrong. When I sat down with him, he began to tell me of his plans to leave his wife and children for a woman he claimed to have fallen in love with. I spent the next two hours pleading with him not to abandon his wife and children. I tried every approach in the book. I talked to him about how this decision would impact his kids' birthdays, graduations, Christmas mornings, and all the other special days in the years to come. I tried to help him focus on the devastation this would bring to the heart of his wife. I talked about practical things such as child support and alimony.

I even feebly attempted to inform him about what God's Word says about matters like these. I wasn't overly optimistic that approach would have any impact on him, however. You see, this was a man who had gone to church for most of his life. He had heard a thousand sermons. He knew his Bible verses frontward and backward. But he had insulated himself from the transforming work of the Holy Spirit. I left that late night meeting discouraged, not very hopeful this man would change his mind.

A short time later the man requested another meeting. I feared the worst, but when he walked through the door, he actually looked different. He announced that he was reconsidering his relationship with the other woman. He wanted to do the right thing, to go God's way. I asked him what had changed his mind. He said, "This is going to sound a little corny. After we met last time, I got in my car and turned on my radio. I heard a chorus of voices singing, 'Amazing grace, how sweet the sound, that saved a wretch like me.' I had heard that song a thousand times, but for the first time, I felt God's amazing grace deep in my heart."

He explained how he identified himself as the "wretch" in the song. He said, "Here I was shattering my wife's heart, breaking my family apart, defying God's Word, and shunning the counsel of my pastor and other close Christian friends. For the first time, my heart was gripped by the fact that even though I am a wretch, God still loves me." At that decisive moment, this man committed to do whatever he could to rebuild his marriage. Thankfully, he had a godly wife who forgave him and their story has a happy ending.

What was the source of this powerful transformation? A deep understanding of the reality of God's passionate love.

I have a theory. I believe people who live the abundant Christian life, who live on a deeper spiritual plane, who are radically devoted to Christ, who are strong during times of crisis, who have a vibrant faith, who dare to live out on a limb, all have one thing in common: At some point in their lives, they have felt God's love firsthand. And the touch of His loving hand has changed them permanently.

A WIDE ANGLE VIEW

1   Tell about a time you experienced God's love in a deep and personal way.

A BIBLICAL PORTRAIT

Read Isaiah 43:4; John 15:9; Ephesians 3:14–19

2 After reading these passages, finish this statement:
When God thinks about me, He feels . . .

3 What does it mean to be "rooted and established in love" in *one* of these areas:

- Knowing God's love for you
- Expressing your love to God
- Living out God's love in your relationships

SHARPENING THE FOCUS

Read Snapshot "God Says He Loves You!"

GOD SAYS HE LOVES YOU!

You can know God loves you because He has said it! Isaiah 43:4 says, "You are precious and honored in my sight and . . . I love you." God has used many images in the Bible to communicate the depth of His love. He says:

- I love you more than a hen loves her chicks (Matt. 23:37).
- I love you more than a good shepherd loves his sheep (John 10:11–14).
- I love you more than the most compassionate father loves his child (Ps. 103:13).
- I love you more than a nursing mother loves her baby (Isa. 49:15).

4. Each of the images in this snapshot communicate different dynamics of the nature of God's love for you. What do you learn about God's love from each of the following images:

- A hen

- A good shepherd

- A compassionate father

- A nursing mother

5. God could have just said, "I love you!" Instead, He used many different illustrations to drive the point home. Why did God use such creativity in expressing His love for you?

Read Snapshot "God Has Proved His Love for You"

GOD HAS PROVED HIS LOVE FOR YOU

Gary Gilmore shot a motel clerk in Provo, Utah. He was arrested, convicted, and sentenced to be shot before a firing squad. When this news became public, the country went into an uproar over the issue of capital punishment. There was a great outpouring of concern about whether or not Gary Gilmore should be executed. The Supreme Court was petitioned to stay his execution, the American Civil Liberties Union filed a class action suit, and religious groups held all-night prayer vigils. Yet out of the millions of people in the United States, to my knowledge not one person ever offered to take his place. Nobody said, "Let me take the bullets."

There is some truth to the statements "Talk is cheap" and "Actions speak louder than words!" Real love begs for expression. There is no more dramatic way of proving your love for someone than to give your life for them. And that is exactly what Jesus did. He gave His life for us, proving the love of God once and for all. "For God so loved the world that he gave his one and only Son, that whoever believes in him shall not perish but have eternal life" (John 3:16).

6 Describe the kind of love it would take for you to give your life for another person.

How would you feel if you offered an incredible act of sacrifice for someone and they still questioned your love?

7 How can you express your thankfulness for how God has proved His love for you?

15

Read Snapshot "God Continues to Show His Love"

GOD CONTINUES TO SHOW HIS LOVE

If God gave the most precious possession He had to express His great love for you, do you think He will be stingy with His other provisions? Will He withhold the resources you need to live? Will He deprive you of emotional support? Will He keep you from sensing you are a member of His family? Does God get some kind of twisted pleasure in holding His love and provision just out of reach like a carrot on a stick? Of course not!

God says He wants to fill your life until it overflows. Believers who walk in faith, obey God's Word, and surrender to God's leading will tell you they feel God's love flowing into their lives. This does not mean the Christian life is problem-free, nor does it mean we will live without pain and challenges. But it does mean that God's grace and love will continue to pour into our lives on a daily basis. He gives direction from His Word, guidance by His Holy Spirit, Christian brothers and sisters to share our joys and sorrows, and opportunities for a meaningful life. On top of all this, He has promised us a home in heaven forever.

8 How is God's ongoing provision a constant reminder of His love?

What are some of the ways God provides for the needs of His children?

9

How have you experienced the provision of God's resources in your life over the past year?

PUTTING YOURSELF IN THE PICTURE

SAYING IT AND SHOWING IT

Take time in the coming week to express your love to God. First, express your love to Him in words. Be creative. Write a prayer of love, sing a song, write a poem, or find some other form of expression to say, "I Love You, God!" Second, affirm your love for God through some tangible action. Show God you love Him by doing something you know will warm His heart. Break a bad habit, start a good habit, offer time to care for someone in need. God gave up something very precious for you. What can you do to affirm your love for Him?

THINK ABOUT THIS

Take time in the coming days to memorize these two passages and think deeply about how God loves you more than a father or mother ever could:

> As a father has compassion on his children, so the LORD has compassion on those who fear him.
>
> *Psalm 103:13*

> Can a mother forget the baby at her breast and have no compassion on the child she has borne? Though she may forget, I will not forget you!
>
> *Isaiah 49:15*

GOD'S PRESENCE

REFLECTIONS FROM SESSION 1

1. If you spent time this week affirming your love for God through some specific word or act, what did you do? How did it bring you closer to your heavenly Father?
2. If you memorized Psalm 103:13 and Isaiah 49:15, how has reflecting on these passages impacted your experience of God's love?

THE BIG PICTURE

Human beings have an amazing capacity to compartmentalize their lives. We can act one way in a particular situation and respond entirely differently in another. From one moment to the next, we can change dramatically. I have watched good-natured, care-free teenagers turn into a frenzied, stomping mob in an effort to touch the shirttails of their favorite rock stars as the stars pass from their limo to the concert hall.

Business people do the same thing. Men and women who faithfully attend church, who share their lives deeply in small groups, who are moved by the Word of God, whose hearts are genuinely stirred and moved by the Holy Spirit, change on Monday morning. They crawl out of bed, calmly climb into business attire, and begin preparing themselves for the war zone they call the office. Throughout the week, they beat down the helpless, intimidate the competition, and attack each other with a vengeance.

It is amazing how human beings can segregate their lives this way. It is even more amazing how Christians can do it. How can Christians act one way in God's house and act another way in the shopping mall, marketplace, ball field, or in the halls at school? I think our ability to live this way is based on a fundamental misunderstanding. Many of us still think God lives in a building. We behave a certain way in church because we have a sense that God is there, so we had better be on our best behavior.

The truth is, if we have received Jesus Christ as Savior, God has taken up residency in a different building—us. The Bible says the building God lives in is our body, our life, our heart. He goes with us wherever we go. He hears every conversation we have. He is a part of every activity we engage in. He is with us at the blue-light special, in the marketplace, on the golf course, in the theater, at school, and everywhere else we go. God loves us so much that He can't stand to love us from a distance. In His love, He has arranged a way to be with us all the time.

A WIDE ANGLE VIEW

1 Describe a time you saw someone go through a radical transformation from one situation to another.

A BIBLICAL PORTRAIT

Read Matthew 27:35–54

2 What are the different ways Jesus suffered as He was being crucified?

3 The curtain of the temple being torn in two was a sign that the way to God was open. How is Jesus' death on the cross the doorway to eternal life?

SHARPENING THE FOCUS

Read Snapshot "Companionship"

COMPANIONSHIP

What benefits does God's presence afford you? The first benefit is companionship. In an overcrowded, overpopulated world, there are still many lonely people. People drive on congested freeways, work in busy office buildings, and interact with many acquaintances, but in the midst of the crowd, they are still desperately seeking meaningful companionship.

Before Jesus returned to heaven, He gave comfort to His followers by saying, "... I am with you always, to the very end of the age" (Matt. 28:20). In Hebrews 13:5 we hear the encouraging words, "Never will I leave you; never will I forsake you." And David knew the power of God's personal presence when he wrote, "Even though I walk through the valley of the shadow of death, I will fear no evil, for you are with me; your rod and your staff, they comfort me" (Ps. 23:4).

Jesus taught His followers about how God would provide His companionship and presence after He returned to heaven. He said, "... I will ask the Father, and he will give you another Counselor to be with you forever—the Spirit of truth. The world cannot accept him, because it neither sees him nor knows him. But you know him, for he lives with you and will be in you" (John 14:16–17).

---

4 How have you experienced the companionship of God through the presence of the Holy Spirit in *one* of these areas:

- In your home life
- In your professional life
- In gathered community worship
- In a friendship
- In a time of struggle or suffering

5 Jesus promised us that when the Holy Spirit came, it would be like having Jesus walk with us every moment of our day. If you knew Jesus was going to appear physically and would walk with you through the coming week, what would change in your schedule?

Although not physically, Jesus will be with you this week through the presence of the Spirit. Why doesn't this reality have the same impact?

Read Snapshot "Conviction"

CONVICTION

God's presence is a two-edged sword. It feels good to know He is with us forever. His companionship is deeply appreciated by all who are fully devoted followers of Christ. But there is also an uncomfortable conviction that comes with knowing He hears every conversation, watches every activity, and knows every thought that passes through our minds.

In Psalm 139 we read, "O Lord, you have searched me and you know me. You know when I sit and when I rise; you perceive my thoughts from afar. You discern my going out and my lying down; you are familiar with all my ways. Before a word is on my tongue you know it completely, O Lord. . . . Where can I go from your Spirit? Where can I flee from your presence? If I go up to the heavens, you are there; if I make my bed in the depths, you are there. . . . If I say, 'Surely the darkness will hide me and the light become night around me,' even the darkness will not be dark to you; the night will shine like the day, for darkness is as light to you" (vv. 1–4, 7–8, 11–12).

6

How would you respond to someone making *one* of these comments:

"I never feel conviction or guilt. God has forgiven me for all my sins, so I'm not going to live with some guilt trip. In Christ's grace I never have to feel bad again. Praise the Lord!"

"I'm just rotten. I feel conviction every moment. I know Jesus died for my sins, but I still feel dirty all the time. I guess you could say I am paralyzed by guilt."

7

Describe a time when you were going about your life, minding your own business, and the conviction of the Holy Spirit cut through and opened your eyes to an area of your life that needed to change.

How did you respond to this conviction?

Read Snapshot "Courage"

COURAGE

God's presence gives us companionship and conviction. It also affords us courage. The truth is, everyone needs courage. In order to live as a fully devoted follower of Christ, you will need to tap into the courage that comes from God's presence.

When the apostle Paul was an old man he wrote to a younger pastor named Timothy and told him about a time of great struggle. "At my first defense, no one came to my support, but everyone deserted me. May it not be held against them. But the Lord stood at my side and gave me strength, so that through me the message might be fully proclaimed and all the Gentiles might hear it. And I was delivered from the lion's mouth. The Lord will rescue me from every evil attack and will bring me safely to his heavenly kingdom. To him be glory for ever and ever. Amen" (2 Tim. 4:16–18). Paul drew on this source of his strength and courage again and again throughout his life. So can we.

8 How have you experienced God giving you courage in a difficult situation?

9 What situation are you currently facing in which you need to be filled with the courage that comes through the presence of God?

In what ways can your small group members pray for you and support you as you face this area of need?

PUTTING YOURSELF IN THE PICTURE

SEARCH ME, LORD

Read Psalm 139 slowly and thoughtfully. Ask God to search every corner of your heart. Invite Him to bring conviction in any area where there is still darkness and sin. Ask Him to shine His light in the darkest corners of your heart and to begin to drive out the darkness.

YOU ARE WITH ME!

Sit down with your schedule for the coming week. Reflect on where you will be, who you will be with, and what you will be doing. As you walk through your schedule, invite Jesus to come along. If you dare to, actually say out loud, "Lord, I invite You to sit in the board meeting and hear every word I say" or "God, I invite You to come on my date and be part of everything I do" or "I invite You to follow me around the house all day and watch my attitude and tone as I spend the day caring for the children You have given me."

If you can't invite God to be with you, seriously reconsider if the activity is something you ought to be doing. Remember, whether you invite Him or not, God will be with you in the coming week.

GOD'S POWER

REFLECTIONS FROM SESSION 2

1. If you have begun a regular process of inviting God to search your heart, how has this impacted your prayer life?
2. If you reviewed your schedule for the week and invited Jesus to walk with you through each day, how did this process change what you did this week?

THE BIG PICTURE

I want to open this session by giving you a transformation test. It is intended to determine how many changes you would like to see occur in your life. If you could wave a wand and make things change in your life, how many things would you want to change? This test includes ten straightforward statements that all pertain to various areas of transformation. You determine which statements reflect changes you would like to see happen in your own life. Keep track of how many apply to you:

1. I would like to lose five or more pounds.
2. I would like to get a better grip on my schedule. I often say I am going to do something but I don't get around to it. I would really like to manage my time better.
3. I would like to worry less. I struggle with anxiety and how I handle pressure and I wish I would worry less.
4. I would like to quit smoking.
5. I would like to have the power to end an unhealthy relationship.
6. I would like to stop drinking or reduce my drinking.
7. I would like to be more disciplined in my spending habits. Money burns a hole in my pockets. I see a sale and I can't resist. I wish I could control myself when it comes to finances.

8. I would like to find more time to read my Bible and pray. I wish I had the discipline to build a strong devotional life.
9. I would like to develop a healthier thought life. I wish my mind was not filled with so many unhealthy thoughts.
10. I would like to have better control over my moods. I seem to be up and down, depressed one day and on the mountaintop the next day. I wish I was more emotionally under control.

A WIDE ANGLE VIEW

1 How did you feel while taking this test?

What was one area of desired change that just jumped off the page and struck you?

A BIBLICAL PORTRAIT

Read Ephesians 1:15–23

2 The apostle Paul asks God to grant specific things to those who are followers of Christ. What does he ask God to give to us?

Why are these things needed in the life of a person who follows Christ?

3

One of the things Paul asks God to give us is power. To what is this power compared?

How do you respond to the idea of this kind of power residing inside of you?

SHARPENING THE FOCUS

Read Snapshot "God's Power in Creation"

GOD'S POWER IN CREATION

God does not have a power problem. Some people think God is retired. They envision God as a grandfatherly figure in a rocking chair who is saying, "Oh, my goodness, look at the condition of the world. It is all going to pieces," while He wrings His hands and feels sad. This could not be further from the truth. Go all the way back to the creation of the universe. The book of Genesis records that God simply spoke and the world came into being. He said the word and the sun, moon, and stars appeared on the scene. He scattered the planets all over the universe with a simple flip of the wrist and a snap of His heavenly fingers. He simply issued a command and plant and animal life began. Then there is the miracle of the creation of mankind: living beings with personality, language, energy, creativity, and the ability to relate to God. When we look at all God has created and how He sustains it every moment, we come face to face with His mighty power.

4 Psalm 19:1 says, "The heavens declare the glory of God; the skies proclaim the work of his hands." How do you experience God's power through the created world?

5 What is one place in creation where you personally sense God's presence and power?

Why is this place meaningful to you?

Read Snapshot "God's Power in Miracles"

GOD'S POWER IN MIRACLES

In the Old Testament we read of God parting the waters of the Red Sea, collapsing the walls of Jericho, scattering manna from heaven, producing water from rocks, speaking through burning bushes, closing the mouths of lions, giving Jonah a custom-made submarine to deliver him to Nineveh, giving victory in battle despite overwhelming odds, and performing countless other miracles. Again and again God displayed His mighty power and strength through earth-shaking miracles. In the New Testament we learn of stars leading wise men to a manger where a virgin delivered a baby. We also read about blind people receiving sight, lame people walking, leprous people receiving healing, the dead being raised, and the list just keeps on going! Our God is powerful and has revealed His power through miracles.

6 What is one Bible story about a miracle that reminds you of the great power of God?

7 How have you seen God work in a miraculous way in your life or in the life of someone you know?

Read Snapshot "God Has Not Changed!"

GOD HAS NOT CHANGED!

The same God who rose Jesus from the grave rules today. The same Jesus who healed and worked miracles is alive. In Hebrews 13:8 we read, "Jesus Christ is the same yesterday and today and forever." God has not changed; only our understanding of Him has changed. God still answers our prayers. He still gives strength to those who are weak. His Spirit continues to comfort those who are grieving. God has power to give hope to the hopeless. In His greatest act of power, God continues to offer forgiveness to sinful people who confess their wrongs and ask for His salvation. There is no power problem in heaven. God is still in charge, and He is more powerful than we could ever imagine.

8 Describe a time in your life when you felt powerless, but the power of God filled you and carried you through.

What would you say to a person who is feeling powerless to overcome an area of sin in his or her life?

9

What is one area in your life in which you need to feel and experience a breakthrough of God's power?

How can your small group members pray for you and support you in this area?

PUTTING YOURSELF IN THE PICTURE

PRAISING GOD FOR HIS POWER

When we focus our prayers on praising God for specific characteristics or qualities He possesses, we often praise God for His holiness, grace, love, and forgiveness, but we neglect to praise Him for His power. Use the space below to write out some prayers of praise for God's power in the following areas:

- Praises for God's power seen in creation:

- Praises for God's power through His miraculous acts (through history and today):

- Praises for the presence of the Holy Spirit in your life giving you power to live each day for Jesus:

PRAYING FOR POWER

Take time in the coming week to identify one or two areas where you need to experience a release of God's power in your life. You may want to use the ten statements in the test at the beginning of this session to give you some ideas. Pray each day for God's power in your life in these areas. Ask God to begin filling you with power to change as well as a deeper conviction of the need to change.

GOD'S PLAN

REFLECTIONS FROM SESSION 3

1. If you have been praising God for His power in creation, how has this opened your eyes to seeing Him more clearly?
2. How have you been experiencing God's power in your life over the past days?

THE BIG PICTURE

Almost everybody has something in their life they would love to change. When we try and fail, our self-esteem takes a beating. Neon lights in our minds flash "failure, failure, failure, failure." God does not want us to live like that. In John 8:31–32 Jesus said, "If you hold to my teaching, you are really my disciples. Then you will know the truth, and the truth will set you free." Jesus wants us to be free from every chain that would bind us, from every negative pattern and stubborn habit that defeats us. He has the power, and He wants to share it with us.

Sadly, many people fall prey to what I call "bumper sticker theology." They build a whole doctrine on a phrase they have seen on a fender of a car. Do you know what one of those phrases is? "Let go and let God." Doesn't that saying paint the picture of someone who believes transformation is entirely God's responsibility? All we have to do is pray, "God, please change this habit or remove this stubborn pattern. Set me from the chains that bind me. If you really love me, do something!"

People who approach God with this mentality assume transformation of human behavior is totally God's business. They don't have to do anything—it's God's job to change their life. When these people don't experience a dramatic release from their struggles when they "Let go and let God," they wrongfully assume that it is not God's will for them to be set free.

Then there are some people who believe that transformation is all up to them. They realize they are saved by grace, but they think they must bring about personal transformation through human effort alone. They picture God saying, "I saved you. The least you can do is clean up your act. Now get moving!"

The truth of the matter is that neither of these extremes is the true biblical pattern for human transformation. God teaches us that transformation is a cooperative venture. He plays an essential part in the process and so do we. God provides us with His Holy Spirit, who gives us the *desire* and *power* to change. God gives us His Word that gives specific direction for change. And God also provides us with Christian brothers and sisters who will assist us in the change process. All of these things help move us toward transformation.

Next, God invites us to cooperate with Him. He asks us to make a commitment to human transformation. We are to exercise self-discipline, put out effort, harness the powers of the human will, and persevere. By working in partnership with us in this way, God builds character into our lives.

A WIDE ANGLE VIEW

1 How have you experienced God's transforming power in *one* of these areas:

- Learning to love a child
- Growing to love and serve a spouse
- Being faithful to do your work in a Christ-honoring way
- Caring for the body God has given you
- Deepening your commitment to grow through Bible study and prayer

How have you needed to work and use your own abilities to grow in that area?

A BIBLICAL PORTRAIT

Read Haggai 1:2–2:9

2 God called His people to rebuild the temple so they could reestablish worship. Use the space below to write down each time you see God's part in the project as well as the part God's people played in rebuilding the temple.

God's Part in the   *The People's Part in*
Building Project   *the Building Project*

● _____   ● _____

● _____   ● _____

● _____   ● _____

● _____   ● _____

● _____   ● _____

3 How do you see God and His people working in cooperation to accomplish the goal of building the temple?

How does this example carry over to how we cooperate with God in bringing about transformation in our lives?

SHARPENING THE FOCUS

Read Snapshot "Developing a Motivation Package"

DEVELOPING A MOTIVATION PACKAGE

The first ingredient in the change process is developing a motivation package. This is a list of reasons or motivations that help compel us to take the first step towards significant change. The key is to sit down with a blank piece of paper and to begin writing down all the factors that might motivate you to change in a specific area of your life. Think of those positive things that will come because of the change. Also, reflect on the negative things that you want to get rid of. Make the list as long and extensive as possible and put it somewhere you will see it often. Keep this "package" in the front of your mind as you prepare to seek transformation in this area of your life.

4 Take time as a group to develop a motivation package that would help a person seek transformation in *one* of the following areas:

- To lose weight
- To develop a habit of daily time with God in Bible study and prayer
- To break off an unhealthy and immoral relationship
- To quit smoking
- To handle finances responsibly

5 Take a few minutes on your own to develop a motivation package in an area of your life in which you are seeking transformation:

Area:

Motivation package:

If I experience transformation in this area, the positive results will be:

- _____

- _____

- _____

If I don't see transformation, some of the negative results will be:

- _____

- _____

- _____

How can developing a motivation package help in the process of seeking personal transformation in your life?

Read Snapshot "Finding a Workable Plan"

FINDING A WORKABLE PLAN

I think most of us are a little naïve with respect to what it takes to actually break the chains of a bad habit. We think we can develop patterns over ten, fifteen, or twenty years and then just change those habits overnight. The truth is, even with a clear motivation package in front of us, bad habits just don't want to cooperate. Couples who have been in a state of marital demise for ten years can't expect three sessions with a marriage counselor to solve all their problems. In the same way, a person who has been addicted to alcohol for years can't just throw away the bottles and expect their desire to drink to go away with the trash. We need a plan, a process for change.

6 Discuss a possible plan to help work toward transformation in *one* of these areas:

- Losing ten pounds and getting in shape
- Committing yourself to grow in your personal devotional life
- Breaking off an unhealthy relationship
- Quitting the smoking habit
- Handling your finances responsibly

Why is a workable plan needed in addition to a motivation package?

7 What are some items that could be part of a workable plan for you to seek transformation for the area you identified in question five?

Read Snapshot "Building in Accountability"

BUILDING IN ACCOUNTABILITY

If you think you can change dramatically all on your own, you are deceived. Human beings aren't built that way. God created us to live in community. He wants us to challenge each other, motivate each other, and hold each other accountable. Proverbs 27:17 says, "As iron sharpens iron, so one man sharpens another." A key element of God's plan for our transformation is to build accountability into our lives.

8

How can your small group members support you and keep you accountable as you seek transformation in your life?

Read Snapshot "A Close Walk with God"

A CLOSE WALK WITH GOD

One final, essential element in God's plan for our personal transformation is consistent spiritual growth. A close, personal, vibrant walk with the Lord is the key to all of this. A desire to please Him becomes the most powerful form of motivation in our motivation package. When we begin growing as fully devoted followers of Christ, we find our hearts crying, "Just say the word, Lord!" Our deepest desire is to live for Him.

9

What can you do to deepen your spiritual life and walk more closely with Christ?

PUTTING YOURSELF IN THE PICTURE

WORKING THE PLAN

Take time in the coming week to go through this four-step plan for walking in the power of God. If you have not already done so, identify one specific area. Then:

1

Form a motivation package.

God's Part   *My part*

- _____   • _____

- _____   • _____

- _____   • _____

- _____   • _____

- _____   • _____

2

Establish a workable plan.

Elements of my plan:

- _____

- _____

- _____

3

Find an accountability person to pray for you and ask you how you are doing on a regular basis.

My accountability person will be:

_____

4

Commit yourself to daily time in God's Word and prayer.

Amount of time I will spend in Bible study daily: _____

Amount of time I will spend in prayer: _____

GOD'S PURPOSE

REFLECTIONS FROM SESSION 4

1. If you have been using the four-step process of transformation you learned in the last session, how has this impacted the specific area you are seeking to change?
2. Which of the four steps do you find most difficult? In what ways can your group members pray for you and encourage you as you continue to seek transformation in this area of your life?

THE BIG PICTURE

Some people believe God's purpose for their life is to give them everything they want. There are pastors and entire congregations that run on this basic concept. These people say God's grand purpose is to bring all of the powers of heaven into action for the sake of making them healthy, wealthy, and happy. In other words, God's primary purpose is to make His children comfortable, prosperous, and problem-free. This kind of teaching is very popular these days, and you will be hearing it more and more in the years to come. Beware of it.

Others believe all they have to do is lead a life of faith, speak the word, claim the promise, or bind the Evil One and God will be compelled to do what they say. This thinking reduces the sovereign God to a divine errand boy, obligated to cater to our wishes.

A third group consists of those who believe God's primary purpose is not comfort, but conflict. God desires to bring hardship into their lives. "You're in the army now soldier, so shape up!" is their battle cry. If you have not run into these people yet, you will. They are absolutely convinced that God's primary purpose for His children is to determine the worst punishment or life situation and inflict it on them mercilessly. They live with the constant fear that God will call them to go and do the very thing that terrifies them the most.

And still others believe that being a Christian means all the joy, fun, and thrills of life will come to a screeching halt. They view God's purpose as being the ultimate cosmic killjoy, the divine party crasher. They are absolutely convinced God is going to see what they enjoy and tell them to knock it off. Then He is going to identify those things which are boring and unfulfilling and assign those tasks to them forever.

All four of these views of God are warped and wrong. God's purposes for His children are so much different than any of these outlooks.

A WIDE ANGLE VIEW

1   What is wrong with these various views of God's purpose for His children?

If a seeker asked you, "If I became a follower of Christ, what would God have planned for me?" What would you say?

Read Romans 8:28–39; Ephesians 2:4–10

In Romans 8:29 we read that we are "to be conformed to the likeness of his Son." What does a person who is "conformed to the likeness of his Son" look like?

3 Take what you learn from these two passages and write a purpose statement:

God's purpose for me is . . .

What do you learn about God's purpose for your life from these two passages?

SHARPENING THE FOCUS

Read Snapshot "Ears Like Jesus"

EARS LIKE JESUS

How are your ears? God wants you to have ears like Jesus had. Jesus had the ability to hear the whisper of His Father's will above the roar of the masses. God wants you to tune into the whisper of the Holy Spirit. He wants you to be able to discern the leading of the Spirit, even through the deafening roar of humanity all around you. God's purpose is for you to become more like your Savior. This means learning to listen like He did.

---

4 What are some noises or distractions that get in the way of hearing God's voice?

What can you do to start tuning out some of this noise and static?

5 What are some of the ways God speaks to His children?

What can you do to be more open to these forms of communication?

Read Snapshot "Mouths Like Jesus"

MOUTHS LIKE JESUS

Jesus made it a habit to build people up with His words. If we want to be more like Him, we need to learn to do the same. This can happen by encouraging others and committing to speak the truth in a loving way. How many marriages break down because communication ceases? Many spouses do not live with a commitment to be an encourager. How many partnerships in businesses disintegrate when people stop affirming each other? How many friendships would find new life if we committed ourselves to use our words to build each other up? First Thessalonians 5:11 says, "Encourage one another and build each other up." This should become our life motto!

---

6 Tell your group about a person in your life who has consistently spoken words of encouragement to you.

How do their words reflect the presence of Christ in their heart?

7 How can you use your words in the coming week to show someone that Jesus Christ is in your life?

Read Snapshot "Hands Like Jesus"

HANDS LIKE JESUS

Jesus' hands were calloused. His hands helped Jesus earn His living as a carpenter. His hands fed the hungry, gave to the poor, touched lepers, and blessed children. His hands gripped the whip to drive impostors out of the house of God. His hands held a wooden cross while His weary feet struggled up a lonely hill of Golgotha. His hands tore and bled for men, women, and children who had hard hearts toward Him. How would you like to have hands like that? God wants you to have hands like Jesus.

---

8 As you think about some of the things Jesus did with His hands, what can you learn from His example?

9 What is one act of service you can commit to do with your hands in the coming week?

How can your group members keep you accountable to follow through on this commitment?

PUTTING YOURSELF IN THE PICTURE

MOUTHS LIKE JESUS

Make a commitment to use your mouth to build others up in the coming week. Make a list of three to six people you know who could use a word of encouragement. Pray for Jesus to speak through you and give you the right words to say to them. Then get on the phone and begin calling through your list. Be very specific with each person you call. Remind each of them of what they mean to you and of how much God loves them. Affirm them for who God is making them to be. Seek to speak with the mouth of Jesus.

SCRIPTURE STUDY

Take time this week to memorize and reflect on the meaning of Ephesians 2:10:

> For we are God's workmanship, created in Christ Jesus to do good works, which God prepared in advance for us to do.

As you grow in your understanding of God's purpose in your life, what are some of the good works God has prepared for you to do?

GOD'S PROMISES

REFLECTIONS FROM SESSION 5

1. Some of you committed to contact three to six people and encourage them with your words. How did people respond to your efforts to show the love of Jesus in this way?
2. If you memorized and reflected on Ephesians 2:10, how has this passage helped you understand God's purpose for your life?

THE BIG PICTURE

God desires to set you free from the chains that bind you! Over the past five sessions we have focused on some amazing truths. God has done many things to help you discover freedom.

The first great truth associated with the Christian faith is that God loves you more than you will ever know. You are His *passion.* If God's love remains only head knowledge, you will probably never come to know Christ in a personal way. But when you realize God loves you passionately, His love grabs your heart forever.

The second great truth we have studied is that God loves you so much He can't stand loving you from a distance. So, through the ministry of His Holy Spirit, He has taken up residence in your life. He has afforded you the great gift of His *presence.* When you commit yourself to be a devoted follower of Christ, you will never be alone again. There will always be someone who understands you. He will never leave you or forsake you.

The third great truth is that there is no power shortage in heaven. The awesome *power* that scattered the stars throughout the galaxies and put the mountains and oceans into place is still active and is available to you for the purposes of transformation. With God's power, you can break every chain that binds you, every stubborn habit, every destructive pattern, every defeating activity, and every unhealthy relationship.

The fourth truth we have learned is that God has a *plan* for accomplishing His transforming work in us. God does not simply wave a magic wand and change every area of struggle in our lives. Nor does He require us to change without His help. Transformation is a cooperative venture. God provides essential ingredients, and so do we. We need to put together a motivation package, establish a workable plan, invite accountability, and commit ourselves to continuing spiritual growth. This is God's plan for working transformation in our lives.

The fifth truth we focused on was that God's *purpose* is for us to become more like His Son, Jesus Christ. God does not promise heaven on earth with no struggles. Neither does He call us to a life of endless suffering and sadness. His design is for us to experience dynamic and radical transformation as we are conformed more and more into the character of Jesus.

In this session, we will focus on two *promises* God has given: (1) A promise of a meaningful and abundant life on this earth, and (2) a promise of an eternal home in heaven. These are just two among literally hundreds of promises recorded in the Bible. When we get a grip on the truth of these promises, they help set us free from the chains that bind us.

A WIDE ANGLE VIEW

1   What is one promise God made in His Word that gives you a sense of freedom?

How does it feel to know God always keeps His promises?

Read John 10:7–10; 14:1–6

2 In John 10 we read of a contrast between the thief and the shepherd. Who is the thief and who is the shepherd?

What are the goals of each?

Jesus said, "I have come that they may have life, and have it to the full." What does Jesus mean by a "full" life?

3 How would you describe the promise Jesus gives in John 14?

According to this passage, how can we know if this promise is for us?

SHARPENING THE FOCUS

Read Snapshot "Experiencing God's Blessing in this Life"

EXPERIENCING GOD'S BLESSING IN THIS LIFE

God has given us a promise. The promise is that while we are still living this life, He will give us a quality of life here on this earth that is full and meaningful. Psalm 23:6 says "Surely goodness and mercy shall follow me all the days of my life ..." (KJV) God wants to set us free from the chains that bind us and free us to experience His presence and blessing in our lives.

God never said His children would be spared from the harsh realities of life. Just because we receive Christ as our Leader and Forgiver, we are not guaranteed a painless existence. We will still face trials, difficulties, and temptations. But after we enter a relationship with Jesus Christ, we live with the power of a promise—a promise that, in spite of our trials, difficulties, and adversities, we will experience God's love. His presence will be felt and His power will be made available. God will continue to transform us into all He wants us to be.

4
How have you experienced God's "goodness and mercy" during a difficult time in your life?

5
Respond to *one* of these statements:

- *"When I am having hard times and struggles, I don't feel any of God's goodness or mercy."*
- *"I have been a follower of Christ for a number of years now and I still don't feel like I am experiencing the Christian life 'to the full.'"*
- *"I would like to experience abundant life in Christ, but to tell the truth, I don't feel worthy to receive His good gifts in my life."*

6 What is one area of your life in which you long to experience a fuller sense of God's purpose and direction?

How can your small group members pray for you as you seek to experience fullness of life in this area?

Read Snapshot "Experiencing God's Blessings Forever"

EXPERIENCING GOD'S BLESSINGS FOREVER

The Bible says that someday everyone who believes in Jesus will be transported to an existence where there will never be tears, sorrow, pain, defeat, humiliation, guilt, or fear. This is a categorical promise from God to every single person who has called on Jesus to be their Savior. Someday the battles of this life will be over. Those who have repented of their sins and acknowledged Jesus Christ as their only hope and leader will spend eternity in the presence of Christ.

7 How does the hope of heaven impact you at *one* of these times:

- When you are facing long days and weeks of struggle and sadness
- When you are walking through the death of a loved one who knew Christ as Savior
- When you grow weary of resisting a recurring sin in your life
- When you are tired of serving in an area of ministry where God has called you

PUTTING YOURSELF IN THE PICTURE

SEEING GOD'S GOODNESS

Sometimes we grow so used to God's goodness in this life that we take it for granted. Take time in the coming week to write down some of the ways you have received God's goodness in your life in the following areas:

- God has shown His goodness by providing for my physical needs. I have . . .
- God has shown His goodness by providing for my relational needs. Some significant people in my life are . . .
- God has shown His goodness by providing for my spiritual needs. God has given me many spiritual blessings, including . . .

Take time to thank God for the richness of His provision. Also, seek to develop a habit of remembering just how much God has given so that you can experience a full life in Christ.

SHARING WHAT YOU HAVE

If you are a follower of Christ, you have the promise of heaven. Take time in the coming week to pray for people in your life who do not yet live with this hope. Pray for courage and an opportunity to tell others about the hope you have because of your faith in Jesus Christ.

LEADER'S NOTES

Leading a Bible discussion—especially for the first time—can make you feel both nervous and excited. If you are nervous, realize that you are in good company. Many biblical leaders, such as Moses, Joshua, and the apostle Paul, felt nervous and inadequate to lead others (see, for example, 1 Cor. 2:3). Yet God's grace was sufficient for them, just as it will be for you.

Some excitement is also natural. Your leadership is a gift to the others in the group. Keep in mind, however, that other group members also share responsibility for the group. Your role is simply to stimulate discussion by asking questions and encouraging people to respond. The suggestions listed below can help you to be an effective leader.

PREPARING TO LEAD

1. Ask God to help you understand and apply the passage to your own life. Unless that happens, you will not be prepared to lead others.
2. Carefully work through each question in the study guide. Meditate and reflect on the passage as you formulate your answers.
3. Familiarize yourself with the Leader's Notes for each session. These will help you understand the purpose of the session and will provide valuable information about the questions in the session. The Leader's Notes are not intended to be read to the group. These notes are primarily for your use as a group leader and for your preparation. However, when you find a section that relates well to your group, you may want to read a brief portion or encourage them to read this section at another time.
4. Pray for the various members of the group. Ask God to use these sessions to make you better disciples of Jesus Christ.
5. Before the first session, make sure each person has a study guide. Encourage them to prepare beforehand for each session.

LEADING THE SESSION

1. Begin the session on time. If people realize that the session begins on schedule, they will work harder to arrive on time.
2. At the beginning of your first time together, explain that these sessions are designed to be discussions, not lectures. Encourage everyone to participate, but realize some may be hesitant to speak during the first few sessions.
3. Don't be afraid of silence. People in the group may need time to think before responding.
4. Avoid answering your own questions. If necessary, rephrase a question until it is clearly understood. Even an eager group will quickly become passive and silent if they think the leader will do most of the talking.
5. Encourage more than one answer to each question. Ask, "What do the rest of you think?" or "Anyone else?" until several people have had a chance to respond.
6. Try to be affirming whenever possible. Let people know you appreciate their insights into the passage.
7. Never reject an answer. If it is clearly wrong, ask, "Which verse led you to that conclusion?" Or let the group handle the problem by asking them what they think about the question.
8. Avoid going off on tangents. If people wander off course, gently bring them back to the passage being considered.
9. Conclude your time together with conversational prayer. Ask God to help you apply those things that you learned in the session.
10. End on time. This will be easier if you control the pace of the discussion by not spending too much time on some questions or too little on others.

We encourage all small group leaders to use *Leading Life-Changing Small Groups* (Zondervan) by Bill Donahue and the Willow Creek Small Group Team while leading their group. Developed and used by Willow Creek Community Church, this guide is an excellent resource for training and equipping followers of Christ to effectively lead small groups. It includes valuable information on how to utilize fun and creative relationship-building exercises for your group; how to plan your meeting; how to share the leadership load by identifying, developing, and working with an "apprentice leader"; and how to find creative ways to do group prayer. In addition, the book includes material and tips on handling potential conflicts and difficult personalities, forming group covenants, inviting new members, improving listening skills, studying the Bible, and much more. Using *Leading Life-Changing Small Groups* will help you create a group that members love to be a part of.

Now let's discuss the different elements of this small group study guide and how to use them for the session portion of your group meeting.

THE BIG PICTURE

Each session will begin with a short story or overview of the lesson theme. This is called "The Big Picture" because it introduces the central theme of the session. You will need to read this section as a group or have group members read it on their own before discussion begins. Here are three ways you can approach this section of the small group session:

- As the group leader, read this section out loud for the whole group and then move into the questions in the next section, "A Wide Angle View." (You might read the first week, but then use the other two options below to encourage group involvement.)
- Ask a group member to volunteer to read this section for the group. This allows another group member to participate. It is best to ask someone in advance to give them time to read over the section before reading it to the group. It is also good to ask someone to volunteer, and not to assign this task. Some people do not feel comfortable reading in front of a group. After a group member has read this section out loud, move into the discussion questions.
- Allow time at the beginning of the session for each person to read this section silently. If you do this, be sure to allow enough time for everyone to finish reading so they can think about what they've read and be ready for meaningful discussion.

A WIDE ANGLE VIEW

This section includes one or more questions that move the group into a general discussion of the session topic. These questions are designed to help group members begin discussing the topic in an open and honest manner. Once the topic of the lesson has been established, move on to the Bible passage for the session.

A BIBLICAL PORTRAIT

This portion of the session includes a Scripture reading and one or more questions that help group members see how the theme of the session is rooted and based in biblical teaching. The Scripture reading can be handled just like "The Big Picture" section: You can read it for the group, have a group member read it, or allow time for silent reading. Make sure everyone has a Bible or that you have Bibles available for those who need them. Once you have read the passage, ask the question(s) in this section so that group members can dig into the truth of the Bible.

Sharpening the Focus

The majority of the discussion questions for the session are in this section. These questions are practical and help group members apply biblical teaching to their daily lives.

Snapshots

The "Snapshots" in each session help prepare group members for discussion. These anecdotes give additional insight to the topic being discussed. Each "Snapshot" should be read at a designated point in the session. This is clearly marked in the session as well as in the Leader's Notes. Again, follow the same format as you do with "The Big Picture" section and the "Biblical Portrait" section: Either you read the anecdote, have a group member volunteer to read, or provide time for silent reading. However you approach this section, you will find these anecdotes very helpful in triggering lively dialogue and moving discussion in a meaningful direction.

Putting Yourself in the Picture

Here's where you roll up your sleeves and put the truth into action. This portion is very practical and action-oriented. At the end of each session there will be suggestions for one or two ways group members can put what they've just learned into practice. Review the action goals at the end of each session and challenge group members to work on one or more of them in the coming week.

You will find follow-up questions for the "Putting Yourself in the Picture" section at the beginning of the next week's session. Starting with the second week, there will be time set aside at the beginning of the session to look back and talk about how you have tried to apply God's Word in your life since your last time together.

PRAYER

You will want to open and close your small group with a time of prayer. Occasionally, there will be specific direction within a session for how you can do this. Most of the time, however, you will need to decide the best place to stop and pray. You may want to pray or have a group member volunteer to begin the lesson with a prayer. Or you might want to read "The Big Picture" and discuss the "Wide Angle View" questions before opening in prayer. In some cases, it might be best to open in prayer after you have read the Bible passage. You need to decide where you feel an opening prayer best fits for your group.

When opening in prayer, think in terms of the session theme and pray for group members (including yourself) to be responsive to the truth of Scripture and the working of the Holy Spirit. If you have seekers in your group (people investigating Christianity but not yet believers), be sensitive to your expectations for group prayer. Seekers may not yet be ready to take part in group prayer.

Be sure to close your group with a time of prayer as well. One option is for you to pray for the entire group. Or you might allow time for group members to offer audible prayers that others can agree with in their hearts. Another approach would be to allow a time of silence for one-on-one prayers with God and then to close this time with a simple "Amen."

GOD'S PASSIONATE LOVE

ISAIAH 43:4; JOHN 15:9; EPHESIANS 3:14—19

INTRODUCTION

We've all seen buttons and badges that say, "Smile, God loves you." We've heard slogans and sung Sunday school songs and hymns—all expressing the fact that God loves us. But no matter how much we've heard it, said it, or sung about it, nothing significant happens in our lives until we *feel* God's love. What we know in our heads must move into our hearts. We need to experience the passionate love of God.

When you feel God's love for the first time, you will find yourself living with a sense of wonder and worship. We are all painfully aware of what goes on in the dark recesses of our lives. I have discovered that the more I grow in Christ, the greater my wonder is that God could love someone like me. Yet the Bible says God knows you and loves you. It even goes so far as to say that every single hair on your head is numbered. God is saying, "I know everything there is to know about you and I still love you."

THE BIG PICTURE

Take time to read this introduction with the group. There are suggestions for how this can be done in the beginning of the leader's section.

A WIDE ANGLE VIEW

Question One There is no right or wrong answer to this question. It might be easy for some to answer and difficult for others. However, it will move you into honest reflection on how various group members have experienced, or have not experienced, God's love.

A BIBLICAL PORTRAIT

Read Isaiah 43:4; John 15:9; Ephesians 3:14–19

Question Two Isaiah 43:4 says you are precious in God's sight. Every one of you. You are precious to Him. We need to face the profound truth that God has actually said it. He has said it from cover to cover in the Bible. Our job is to believe it, to accept it, to rejoice in it. We need to claim it and hold on to it with all our strength. We have to let it touch our hearts. We must keep this message from getting mentally processed and then discarded. We need to say out loud, "God loves me."

In John 15:9 Jesus tells us that He loves us just as much as His heavenly Father loves Him. Stop and try to grasp the importance of this statement. How much does God the Father love His only Son, Jesus? That is how much Jesus loves us! We need to accept this truth, to rejoice in it, and to live as beloved children of God.

In Ephesians 3:19 the apostle Paul said that Christ's love for you surpasses knowledge. In other words, your mind can't begin to understand the depth of His love for you. It is too deep, too high, too wide for you to completely grasp. But He still wants you to know it, so He said it out loud!

Question Three God has declared His love for us. He also calls us to respond by living lives of love for Him. Think about the "Great Commandment:"

> "Teacher, which is the greatest commandment in the Law?"
> Jesus replied: "'Love the Lord your God with all your heart and
> with all your soul and with all your mind.' This is the first and
> greatest commandment. And the second is like it: 'Love your
> neighbor as yourself.' All the Law and the Prophets hang on
> these two commandments" (Matt. 22:36–40).

We must first receive His love; then, in a response to His great grace, we are called to love Him and others. What does a mature follower of Christ look like when they are "rooted and established in love?" Take time as a group to reflect on what characteristics mark the life of a person who knows the love of God and who allows this love to transform their relationships.

Sharpening the Focus

Read Snapshot "God Says He Loves You" before Question 4

Question Four Each image draws out different aspects of God's love. A hen puts her wing over her young to protect them . . . our God has a protecting love over us. A good shepherd leads sheep to green pastures . . . our God has a providing love for us. A father shows compassion on his children . . . our God has compassion on us. A mother is gentle and tender . . . our God has a tender and sensitive love for His children. The illustrations go on and on. Take time as a group to reflect on the many insights that can be drawn from these images.

Read Snapshot "God Has Proved His Love for You" before Question 6

Question Six Many of us believe God is semi-concerned about us, but too few of us believe He loves us passionately. He loves us to the extent that He would take our place and die for us. He saw us condemned by our sin. He knew we were found guilty before the courts of heaven and that we were sentenced to death. He knew that without His radical intervention, we would suffer separation and emptiness in this life as well as punishment and condemnation in the next.

Jesus was arrested, mocked, beaten, spit on, slapped, given a crown of thorns, and nailed to the cross. He hung naked to die a slow and painful death. He did this for one reason and one reason only. He loves us with a passionate love! He couldn't bear to see us suffer separation and the condemnation of hell forever. He took our punishment. He has proved His love for us beyond all doubt!

Occasionally, in a weak moment, a Christian will say to me, "You know, I don't think God really cares about me." It rattles my brain when I hear a comment like this. I feel like asking, "What more could He do? Can you set a standard beyond giving life's blood? What more do you want? The highest standard was met for you. God removed all doubt of His great love for you by dying on the cross." Such a statement reveals more about that person's inability to receive God's love than about what God has done to show it. Something is clearly broken, but not on God's side of the equation.

Try to put yourself in His place. How would you feel if you had given everything, even your own life, and people still said, "I don't think you love me." There is no way God could show His love for us in more graphic way than he already has.

Read Snapshot "God Continues to Show His Love" before Question 8

Question Eight Some people might say, "What about today? What is God doing in human history to show His love in our day and age?" That is a very fair question. To answer it, let me direct you to a powerful verse from the Bible that seems almost too good to be true: "He who did not spare his own Son, but gave him up for us all—how will he not also, along with him, graciously give us all things?" (Rom. 8:32). This passage reminds us that if God didn't spare the life of Jesus in demonstrating His love for you, He certainly won't cut corners when it comes to your provision and ongoing care.

This little story might help drive the point home. You may want to read it for your group as you prepare to discuss questions eight and nine. Suppose a very wealthy friend invited you to a lavish dinner party. He gave you a gold-embossed invitation, sent a chauffeur to pick you up, had a steward open the door and invite you into the home, and sat you down at a table filled with more extravagant food than you had ever seen. Do you think your wealthy friend, who went to all that trouble conveying his love for you, would refuse to give you silverware for the meal? Never.

PUTTING YOURSELF IN THE PICTURE

Tell group members you will be providing time at the beginning of the next meeting for them to discuss how they have put their faith into action. Let them tell their stories. However, don't limit their interaction to the two options provided. They may have put themselves into the picture in some other way as a result of your study. Allow for honest and open communication.

Also, be clear that there will not be any kind of a "test" or forced reporting. All you are going to do is allow time for people to volunteer to talk about how they have applied what they learned in your last study. Some group members will feel pressured if they think you are going to make everyone provide a "report." You don't want anyone to skip the next group because they are afraid of having to say they did not follow up on what they learned from the prior session. Focus instead on providing a place for honest communication without creating pressure and fear of being embarrassed.

Every session from this point on will open with a look back at the "Putting Yourself in the Picture" section of the previous session.

GOD'S PRESENCE

MATTHEW 27:35–54

INTRODUCTION

The second great truth that brings us freedom is that God loves us so much that He couldn't stand to love us from afar. So, He arranged a way for us to experience His presence twenty-four hours a day, 365 days a year. Through the presence of His Holy Spirit, God has taken up permanent residence in our hearts and lives. He is with us wherever we go, whatever we do, whoever we spend time with. God's presence offers us companionship, conviction, and courage. As His followers, we need to grow more and more responsive to His presence as we grow in faith.

THE BIG PICTURE

Take time to read this introduction with the group. There are suggestions for how this can be done in the beginning of the leader's section.

A WIDE ANGLE VIEW

Question One We have all seen this happen. There is a little Dr. Jekyl and Mr. Hyde in all of us. Encourage group members to communicate how they have seen this transformation happen in their own lives or in the life of someone else.

A BIBLICAL PORTRAIT

Read Matthew 27:35–54

Questions Two & Three In the Old Testament, God clearly loved His people. But at that point in redemptive history, God loved His people from a distance. He intervened in their lives from time to time, demonstrating His power and love and working miracles. But in general, His presence was not felt in deep, personal ways.

In the New Testament, we see an amazing thing happen. Jesus, the second person of the Trinity, took on human flesh and came one step closer. John 1:14 says God became flesh and lived among us. Now God's personal presence could be seen and touched in the person of Jesus. God, in the form of Jesus Christ, was relating to ordinary people for the first time. We see Him teaching among common folk, fellowshiping among fishermen, healing the broken, feeding people, and blessing children.

However, the curtain in the temple was still a constant reminder that human beings could not approach the presence of God. This was dealt with completely and finally when Jesus died on the cross and the hands of God tore that curtain into two pieces from top to bottom. The way to God was now open through the sacrifice of Jesus. There were no more barriers between God and his people.

From that point on we were invited to come as children into the arms of the Father. In fact, Paul completes this picture of intimacy when he says, "Do you not know that your body is a temple of the Holy Spirit, who is in you, whom you have received from God? You are not your own" (1 Cor. 6:19). Our body is the home of the Holy Spirit. If you know Jesus as your Savior and Lord, God has taken up residence in your life.

SHARPENING THE FOCUS

Read Snapshot "Companionship" before Question 4

Question Four God's presence affords us a quality of companionship no human being can ever offer. So why don't we feel it more often? Many times we don't experience His presence because we don't take Him at His word. This is not an accusation, only an observation. I know many people don't take Him at His word because I listen to how they pray.

I know it is dangerous to make editorial comments about someone else's prayers, but from time to time I think it can be helpful. Too often I hear people praying sloppy prayers. They pray, "Oh, Lord, be with me today." God has already made His promise, "I will be with you always, even to the end of the age. I will never leave you or forsake you. I won't forsake you as orphans. I am with you. I live inside of you. I am not going anywhere." He says it over and over again. He is with you. Take Him at His word.

Why not pray, "Lord, help me live in the awareness of Your presence today. I'll take You at Your word that You are going to be with me. Help me experience Your presence deeply and personally in everything I do. Open my ears to hear You speak. Open my eyes to see You work."

When we respond this way, we will begin to sense God's presence in every area of our lives. To encourage group members in this truth, encourage them to tell about times they have experienced the intimate presence of God in their daily lives.

Question Five Let's face it, if Jesus was physically with us, our whole schedule would turn upside down. Discuss this question and try to sort out why His presence in Spirit does not seem to move us as much as His physical presence would. Encourage your small group members to seek to live each moment of life knowing that His spiritual presence in their hearts is just as real as His physical presence would be. There is a follow-up on this question in the application section of this lesson entitled, "Putting Yourself in the Picture." Be sure to point this out at the end of this session and encourage group members to use this exercise as they plan their week.

Read Snapshot "Conviction" before Question 6

Question Six These two statements take opposite extremes on the issue of conviction. Some people claim they never have to feel guilty again because they are forgiven. They don't feel conviction and are not moved to turn from their sin. This extreme is dangerous. It leads to spiritual immaturity and to continuing sinful behavior. These people need to hear a little more conviction from the Holy Spirit.

On the other hand, there are those who are crushed over personal guilt and conviction. They go beyond the conviction of the Holy Spirit and add ten thousand pounds of life-draining pressure on themselves. They become paralyzed and are crushed under the weight of their own guilt. This is also wrong. The Spirit convicts out of love and in a desire to move us to change. These people need to be reminded of God's love. He wants to help them keep growing, but His love for them has not been removed.

Read Snapshot "Courage" before Question 8

Question Eight When a believer loses a loved one, God will give the courage needed to get up each morning and go on. God also offers courage to those who have lost their jobs . . . no failure with God is final. He will give a salesperson courage to keep on making business calls, even though the last one hundred of them have turned up empty. He will give courage to young mothers to continue doing the repetitive tasks associated with motherhood. He will give courage to those who need to say no to peers who are trying to convince them to do something they know is wrong. He will give courage to those serving in His church even though no one is giving them recognition. He will give people courage to face issues that come up in their sexual life so they can live in a way that is pleasing to Him. God's presence affords courage we could never manufacture on our own.

PUTTING YOURSELF IN THE PICTURE

Challenge group members to take time in the coming week to use part or all of this application section as an opportunity for continued growth.

God's Power

Ephesians 1:15—23

Introduction

No matter how spiritual, intellectual, disciplined, or sophisti-
cated we are, almost all of us can identify areas in our lives we
would give anything to be able to change. So many of us live
with chains that bind us. We don't seem to have the power to
break the chains. But God has an endless surplus of power
that He wants to make available to us. He does not take away
all of our struggles, but he does offer us power so we can resist
and begin working with Him at bringing change in our lives
and breaking the chains that bind us.

God wants to release His power in our lives for the purpose of
transformation. Second Corinthians 5:17 says, "Therefore, if
anyone is in Christ, he is a new creation; the old has gone,
the new has come!" As Christians, we become a whole new
person. All of the old stuff is going to fade away, and we will
learn to utilize God's power. We enter a partnership with God
as we learn to walk in freedom.

The Big Picture

Take time to read this introduction with the group. There are
suggestions for how this can be done in the beginning of the
leader's section.

A Wide Angle View

Question One As a leader, don't ask group members to grade
themselves or say how many questions applied to their life.
Simply give an opportunity for group members to express how
they felt while taking the test. At this point they can volunteer
as much or as little information as they desire. For those who
are feeling a little more bold, the follow-up question will give
them a chance to disclose one area in which they felt some
conviction.

A BIBLICAL PORTRAIT

Read Ephesians 1:15–23

Question Two Paul lifts up a powerful prayer for Christ's followers at the church in Ephesus. These same things should be prayed for all believers. Along with praying for power, Paul asks God to give these Christians a spirit of wisdom, a better understanding of God, eyes that are enlightened, knowledge of the hope they have in Christ, an understanding of the great inheritance they have as saints of God, and an experience of Christ's resurrection power. Reflect on a number of these prayer requests. Why are these still needed in the lives of Christians?

Question Three Paul prays for the same power that raised Jesus from the grave to be at work in the lives of believers. Think about it. What kind of power did it take for Jesus to be raised? What type of victorious power was exercised when Jesus broke free from the chains of death? What amount of power did it take to break the power of sin and the devil and win salvation for all who would believe? It is this same power that is at work in the lives of all those who believe in Jesus. That is serious power!

SHARPENING THE FOCUS

Read Snapshot "God's Power in Creation" before Question 4

Questions Four & Five Take time as a group to reflect on the greatness of God's creation. Every person who has looked at the wonder of God's created world has a sense of His great power. The heavens still scream out the truth that God reigns! The mountains and oceans sing His praises. Think deeply about the revelation of God's power through creation. This same power is at work in all followers of Christ. You see, Jesus, who created the heavens and the earth, dwells in your life.

Read Snapshot "God's Power in Miracles" before Question 6

Question Six There are all sorts of Bible stories that tell about God's miraculous power. Do you remember Daniel in the lions' den? Daniel was tossed to the lions for dinner, but suddenly the lions weren't hungry. Or read the book of Jonah sometime. God appointed a storm to toss Jonah's escape ship around. A little later the crew of the boat threw Jonah over the side and God sent a custom-made fish to swallow him. Three days later God tells the fish to deposit Jonah on the shore near God's intended destination. Working miracles is no problem for God. These are just two of several miracle stories in the Old Testament.

Many such miracles are also seen in the New Testament. Consider the birth of Jesus. What is the first thing God does to lead people to the celebration of the birth of Jesus? He calls a star to point the way to a stable in Bethlehem. Scientists today have a hard enough time studying stars; in their wildest dreams they wouldn't ever try to create or control one. God also causes a supernatural conception in Mary, a young virgin girl who conceived a son by the Holy Spirit. And when Jesus grows up He does healings, causing the blind to see, the lame to walk. We see Him changing water to wine and feeding multitudes of people with just a handful of food. We even see Him raising people from the dead. The greatest miracle of all was when Jesus rose from the dead after giving His life for our sins. Who has that kind of power? The answer is clear . . . God does!

Question Seven Some people say God no longer does miracles. This is simply not true. God continues to heal bodies, hearts, relationships, emotions, and everything He chooses to touch. We don't control God or manipulate Him for our purposes. We also can't claim healing or demand that God must always give us what we ask. However, God still works powerful miracles in the lives of those who follow Him. If you don't believe this, simply listen to the stories told by your group members. Most of them, if they have been followers of Christ for any time, have seen the power of God's hand at work in miraculous ways.

Read Snapshot "God Has Not Changed!" before Question 9

Questions Eight & Nine We all have areas in which we need to experience God's presence and mighty power. As group members communicate an area in their life in which they feel they need a fresh experience of God's power, be sure to take note of these and to pray for them in the coming days.

PUTTING YOURSELF IN THE PICTURE

Challenge group members to take time in the coming week to use part or all of this application section as an opportunity for continued growth.

God's Plan

Haggai 1:2—2:9

Introduction

God has promised to unleash His power in our lives as we
seek transformation to become more like Jesus. However, He
does not do it all for us; He calls us to work in partnership
with Him. In this session we will focus on a straightforward
four-step process for seeking transformation in our lives. It
might help to direct the attention of group members back to
the introduction from session three. Look again at the transformation test and encourage each group member to identify
one specific area of their life in which they desire to experience change. This lesson will make sense only if each group
member focuses on one specific area of life where he or she
feels the Lord wants them to experience transformation.

The Big Picture

Take time to read this introduction with the group. There are
suggestions for how this can be done in the beginning of the
leader's section.

A Wide Angle View

Question One Part of the reason God calls us to participate
in the transformation process is because He is trying to build
character in our life. There is no question that God wants to
see us set free from the chains that bind us. However, He is
also trying to strengthen the fabric of our life and deepen our
roots. He could wave a wand and transform us in an instant,
but that would eventually cause us to be weak, undisciplined,
spoiled, and spineless people. It would also keep us distant
from brothers and sisters who need to see us even with our
faults. He loves us too much to treat us this way. Instead He
says, "I will participate with you in breaking the chains that
bind you, but you are going to have to cooperate with Me.
You are going to have to give up projecting the image that you
have it all together and allow others to see you as weak. We
are going to cut those chains together and you are going to
deepen and build character along the way. By the end of this
growth process, you will be more fit for use in My kingdom.

You will have a stronger backbone and be more able to withstand the harsh realities that stand in your future." In His love, God wants to work with us and His people in partnership.

A Biblical Portrait

Read Haggai 1:2–2:9

Question Two This brief book of the Bible is a wonderful example of partnership with God. The people of Israel had focused only on their own needs and had failed to rebuild the temple. Now God was calling them to action. As you study this passage, notice the way God works with His people in a partnership. Identify what part God took in the project and what He expected the people to do. There are many parallels to how God continues to work in collaboration with His followers.

Sharpening the Focus

Read Snapshot "Developing a Motivation Package" before Question 4

Questions Four & Five As stated in the introduction to this session, the rest of this session will make sense only if each group member identifies one specific area they need to experience transformation. Group members need to integrate the principals about which they have read into a specific area of growth.

There are many examples that you might look at as a group. Here is one example to get you started. I've counseled a number of people over the years who wanted to stop smoking. We sit down in my office or a restaurant and I ask them to take a paper and pencil and form a motivation package. I say, "Let's talk about reasons for not smoking." So we talk about financial reasons for the person to stop smoking. "Have you ever calculated how much one pack of cigarettes costs?" "How many packs do you smoke a day? Per week? Per month? Per year?" We figure out how much that habit costs and write down the hard figures . . . that is a motivation to stop! Then I usually bring some of the articles I have compiled over the years and ask the person to read some of the sections about the physical costs associated with smoking. Then I talk about relational costs. I try everything in the book. I'll ask, "Does your spouse like it when you smoke? Are you ever going to tell your little nine-year-old not to smoke? You know kids have a way of doing what Daddy does, even when he tells them not to. Actions do speak louder than words."

That is what a motivation package is all about. Do you get the point? This works in any area you are seeking transformation. Be sure to look at the negative side if you continue on the wrong path and the positive side if you begin to experience transformation.

Read Snapshot "Finding a Workable Plan" before Question 6

Question Six If you need to get a grip on your budgeting practices, there are Christian organizations that will meet with you and help you put together a budget, financial goals, debt reduction plans, and form a workable plan for transformation in this area of your life. You can get help with your insurance, estate planning, investments, and many other aspects of your financial life. You can even go down to a bookstore and buy books on how to put together a plan for getting your budget under control. The key is, you need to be practical and form a realistic and workable plan.

For those who have drinking problems, there are rehabilitation centers, outpatient counselors, and groups like AA. Any of these plans can work. Those who are fighting a weight problem can draw from countless plans for proper nutrition, diet, and exercise. If you have a problem with anxiety, you can read books, attend seminars, listen to tapes or join a support group. The point is, you need to have a plan. In many cases there are already good programs out there that you can use.

Read Snapshot "Building in Accountability" before Question 8

Question Eight Some years ago, through a series of meetings with doctors, I was convinced that I needed to get very serious about my physical conditioning. It wasn't that I was that much overweight—maybe ten pounds or so—but the problem was that I spent much of my time sitting behind a desk. I was instructed to get on a rigid exercise program. I knew I would never stick to an exercise program unless I had someone who would hold me accountable. To help motivate myself to get to the gym, I found a friend who would meet me there and work out with me four to five times a week. Knowing he would be there and having that built-in accountability kept me from dropping out of my program on more than one occasion.

Read Snapshot "A Close Walk with God" before Question 9

Question Nine Encourage group members to communicate specific goals for personal spiritual growth. Ask them to pray for each other and to keep each other accountable to spend time for personal growth on a regular basis.

PUTTING YOURSELF IN THE PICTURE

Challenge group members to take time in the coming week to use part or all of this application section as an opportunity for continued growth.

GOD'S PURPOSE

ROMANS 8:28–39; EPHESIANS 2:4–10

INTRODUCTION

Human beings were created to be dynamic, not static. Some of us have been bound for so long that the idea of God bringing transformation in our life seems like a foreign concept. You might even be saying, "Could it happen to me?" Yes it can! In fact, that's God's plan. It is what He wants to see happen in our lives. God's ultimate purpose is to conform us into the image of Christ.

But how does this happen? It doesn't happen after a single dramatic prayer. It doesn't happen in a seminary classroom. It doesn't happen during a single, stirring sermon. The process of being conformed into the image of Jesus Christ happens gradually in the everyday trenches of life. It happens as we look at every area of our lives and seek to live the way He lived. In this session we will look at three specific areas in which we can seek to be more like Jesus—how we listen, how we speak, and how we use our hands.

THE BIG PICTURE

Take time to read this introduction with the group. There are suggestions for how this can be done in the beginning of the leader's section.

A WIDE ANGLE VIEW

Question One The goal here is not to put down other churches or pastors, but simply to identify some wrong views. Too often these can creep into our own thinking and poison how we view God. We need to go back to the Bible and see what it says about our purpose for living. Sometimes to identify what is right, we need to first filter out what is wrong.

A BIBLICAL PORTRAIT

Read Romans 8:28–39; Ephesians 2:4–10

Question Two God has a grand purpose for your life. Romans 8:29 says that God's ultimate purpose is neither your comfort nor a lifetime of conflict. The ultimate purpose for your life is for you to be conformed to the image of Jesus Christ, His Son. But what does conformity mean?

In some circles, *conformity* is a four-letter word. I don't particularly like the sound of it myself. Do you know what comes to my mind when I hear the word *conformity*? I think of rows of people mindlessly marching in step, all dressed the same, thinking the same, and acting the same. I think of the eradication of individuality, the loss of personality and spontaneity.

This is not what God means by conformity. He is not interested in conforming you externally. He is not concerned about standardizing personalities or getting rid of your temperament. He is not even interested in conforming you to the acceptable standards of the church.

Instead, God wants you to be *extra*ordinary. He knows your personality, your idiosyncrasies, and your frame. You are fearfully and wonderfully made. God's primary purpose is to save you, free you, empower you, equip you, and instruct you as to how you can have character like that of the most remarkable person who ever lived on this planet—Jesus.

Question Three Rather than listen to the many voices out in the world telling us what our purpose in life is, have group members study these two passages and learn from the Bible. After they have summarized their learning in a brief purpose statement, invite them to read it for the group or to put it in their own words. Encourage group members to put this in the first person: "God's plan for *me* is . . ."

SHARPENING THE FOCUS

Read Snapshot "Ears Like Jesus" before Question 4

Question Four There are many things that can distract us from hearing God's voice—busy schedules, sin in our life, not taking time to be quiet, and many other things. Encourage group members to talk about some of the distractions that block their ears and keep them from hearing God's voice. Think together as a group about how you can get rid of some of the distractions so you can hear God's voice with greater clarity.

Question Five Worship is a great setting to hear God's voice. Every time you gather with other followers of Christ, it is good to pray, "Lord, today we need to hear a word from You. We want You to speak to us through a song or through the message." You need to come with an expectation that you will get a word from God.

God also speaks clearly through His Word, the Bible. The Bible is one of the primary vehicles God uses to communicate His will and direction for our lives. This is why it is so important for followers of Christ to make a commitment to spend time reading God's Word each day. We need to read it and then follow what God says.

God also speaks through the still, small voice of His Spirit. I know it sounds mystical, but those little nudges and convictions we feel are from God. God speaks to His children, from time to time, through His Spirit. Not only do we need to hear those promptings, but we need to make sure they are from God and then act on them.

Read Snapshot "Mouths Like Jesus" before Question 6

Questions Six & Seven A compliment for a small deed of kindness has power beyond what most of us realize. Compliments register deeply. We also need to realize the value of statements of affection. People need to hear us tell them how much they mean to us.

God gives us an example of this kind of verbal affirmation in Isaiah 43, one of my favorite passages in Scripture. God the Father says, in effect, "You are precious in My sight. I have called you by name and you are Mine, I love you." It's good to be reminded that God loves us. But the key is for us to learn from God's example and begin to express words of encouragement, affirmation, and blessing.

Unbelievable power for good can be accomplished when we use our tongues constructively. Encouraging people makes their day. Complimenting them builds them up. If we tell a person how our heart is filled with love for them, we can impact them for a lifetime. God's purpose is for us to become more like Jesus. This means that we need to learn to use our words to build others up.

Read Snapshot "Hands Like Jesus" before Question 8

Question Eight When you stop and think about it, Jesus did many things with His hands. He worked hard as a carpenter. He touched those who were sick and outcast. He fed those who were hungry. He washed the feet of His followers. If we think about what Jesus did with His hands, it is a powerful example for us to follow.

Question Nine Use this opportunity at the close of your group to support each other in being more like Jesus. This is your chance to act on what you have learned and to encourage each other to be more like Jesus.

PUTTING YOURSELF IN THE PICTURE

Challenge group members to take time in the coming week to use part or all of this application section as an opportunity for continued growth.

GOD'S PROMISES
JOHN 10:7—10; JOHN 14:1—6

INTRODUCTION

God has done so much to break the chains that bind us. He has shown us the depth of His passionate love for all who believe in Him. He has given us the presence of His Holy Spirit to fill us, lead us, and strengthen us. He has unleashed His great power in our lives. He has given us a practical plan for how we can take part in the transformation process that needs to happen in our lives. He has also given us a purpose for living. His purpose is for us to become more and more like His Son, Jesus Christ. If all of this were not enough, God has given us many promises that help to set us free. In this study we will focus on two of these promises: We will experience a richness of His blessing in this life, and we have the promise of spending eternity in heaven with our God. We are set free from the chains that held us because Jesus Christ has risen from the dead, conquered death and the devil, and has gone ahead to prepare a place for all who believe in Him.

THE BIG PICTURE

Take time to read this introduction with the group. There are suggestions for how this can be done in the beginning of the leader's section.

A WIDE ANGLE VIEW

Question One Do you realize the power in a promise? A soldier who has been transported to another place promises his wife, "Someday I am going to come home to you and the kids." They write back and forth. They talk on the phone when they can. The soldier gets discouraged because he hates being separated from those he loves. But, there is the promise he will return home someday. The wife is taking care of the home and children but she presses on knowing she received a promise that he is coming back. They both live above the despair because they have a promise that gives them hope.

If we are hopeful because of human promises that sometimes don't become a reality, how much more should we find hope in God's promises. Take time to reflect on some of the promises God has made to all who follow Him.

A BIBLICAL PORTRAIT

Read John 10:7–10; John 14:1–6

Question Two Jesus is drawing out a contrast between Himself and the devil. Jesus' desire is to protect us, provide for us, love us, and lead us to heaven. He wants us to experience a full and abundant life. The thief is the devil, the enemy of our souls. He wants to rob us of joy, strip us of hope, and leave us empty and naked. We need to learn how to keep our eyes fixed on the Good Shepherd and follow Him at all times.

Question Three Jesus Himself promises that He will be going to prepare a place in heaven for all who believe. He also wants us to know that He will be the One to bring us into this eternal paradise. However, He does not say that the doors of heaven are open to everyone without question. Instead, He teaches that He alone is the way to heaven. Only those who have faith in Him and who receive His forgiveness live with the promise of spending eternity with God.

SHARPENING THE FOCUS

Read Snapshot "Experiencing God's Blessing in this Life" before Question 4

Question Four When we experience seasons of despair, we must remember that we still live with a promise. In spite of whatever we face, we face it with the One who loves us beyond description. We confront our struggles with the indwelling presence of the Almighty God who will never leave us or forsake us. We have access to a power that is greater than any other force in the universe. We have purpose and direction for life. God can say that goodness and mercy will follow us all the days of our lives because, even in the middle of the struggles of life, we know we are not alone. Our God is with us.

Question Five Each of these statements shows a lack of understanding about the promise of God's blessing in our lives. If you need to, go back to the two passages in the "Biblical Portrait" section of this session. Seek to give honest and sensitive responses to these statements. Try to give a correct understanding of what it means to live a full and abundant life as a follower of Christ.

Read Snapshot "Experiencing God's Blessings Forever" before Question 7

Question Seven If we could peek behind the curtain of time and get a thirty-second glance of what heaven will be like, we would never be the same. We would tend to interpret all of life's difficulties against the backdrop of what heaven will be like. We would find ourselves echoing the words of the apostle Paul from Romans 8:18, "I consider that our present sufferings are not worth comparing with the glory that will be revealed in us."

We are going to be in eternity a whole lot longer than we are on earth. Some of us tend to focus only on the here and now. God wants us to live above the here and now, and live with the hope of His promise. When you don't think you can hold on, when you don't think you can go the next step, when you feel like you are drowning, God says, "Think of heaven and hold on!"

PUTTING YOURSELF IN THE PICTURE

Challenge group members to take time in the coming week to use part or all of this application section as an opportunity for continued growth.

ADDITIONAL WILLOW CREEK RESOURCES

Small Group Resources

Coaching Life-Changing Small Group Leaders, by Bill Donahue and Greg Bowman
The Complete Book of Questions, by Garry Poole
The Connecting Church, by Randy Frazee
Leading Life-Changing Small Groups, by Bill Donahue and the Willow Creek Team
The Seven Deadly Sins of Small Group Ministry, by Bill Donahue and Russ Robinson
Walking the Small Group Tightrope, by Bill Donahue and Russ Robinson

Evangelism Resources

Becoming a Contagious Christian (book), by Bill Hybels and Mark Mittelberg
The Case for a Creator, by Lee Strobel
The Case for Christ, by Lee Strobel
The Case for Faith, by Lee Strobel
Seeker Small Groups, by Garry Poole
The Three Habits of Highly Contagious Christians, by Garry Poole

Spiritual Gifts and Ministry

Network Revised (training course), by Bruce Bugbee and Don Cousins
The Volunteer Revolution, by Bill Hybels
What You Do Best in the Body of Christ—Revised, by Bruce Bugbee

Marriage and Parenting

Fit to Be Tied, by Bill and Lynne Hybels
Surviving a Spiritual Mismatch in Marriage, by Lee and Leslie Strobel

Ministry Resources

An Hour on Sunday, by Nancy Beach
Building a Church of Small Groups, by Bill Donahue and Russ Robinson
The Heart of the Artist, by Rory Noland
Making Your Children's Ministry the Best Hour of Every Kid's Week, by Sue Miller and
    David Staal
Thriving as an Artist in the Church, by Rory Noland

Curriculum

An Ordinary Day with Jesus, by John Ortberg and Ruth Haley Barton
Becoming a Contagious Christian (kit), by Mark Mittelberg, Lee Strobel, and Bill Hybels
Good Sense Budget Course, by Dick Towner, John Tofilon, and the Willow Creek Team
If You Want to Walk on Water, You've Got to Get Out of the Boat, by John Ortberg with
    Stephen and Amanda Sorenson
The Life You've Always Wanted, by John Ortberg with Stephen and Amanda Sorenson
The Old Testament Challenge, by John Ortberg with Kevin and Sherry Harney, Mindy
    Caliguire, and Judson Poling

Willow Creek Association
Vision, Training, Resources for Prevailing Churches

This resource was created to serve you and to help you build a local church that prevails. It is just one of many ministry tools that are part of the Willow Creek Resources® line, published by the Willow Creek Association together with Zondervan.

The Willow Creek Association (WCA) was created in 1992 to serve a rapidly growing number of churches from across the denominational spectrum that are committed to helping unchurched people become fully devoted followers of Christ. Membership in the WCA now numbers over 10,500 Member Churches worldwide from more than ninety denominations.

The Willow Creek Association links like-minded Christian leaders with each other and with strategic vision, training, and resources in order to help them build prevailing churches designed to reach their redemptive potential. Here are some of the ways the WCA does that.

- **A2: Building Prevailing Acts 2 Churches—Today**—an annual two-and-a-half day event, held at Willow Creek Community Church in South Barrington, Illinois, to explore strategies for building churches that reach out to seekers and build believers, and to discover new innovations and breakthroughs from Acts 2 churches around the country.

- **The Leadership Summit**—a once a year, two-and-a-half-day conference to envision and equip Christians with leadership gifts and responsibilities. Presented live at Willow Creek as well as via satellite broadcast to over one hundred locations across North America, this event is designed to increase the leadership effectiveness of pastors, ministry staff, volunteer church leaders, and Christians in the marketplace.

- **Ministry-Specific Conferences**—throughout each year the WCA hosts a variety of conferences and training events—both at Willow Creek's main campus and offsite, across the U.S., and around the world—targeting church leaders and volunteers in ministry-specific areas such as: evangelism, small groups, preaching and teaching, the arts, children, students, women, volunteers, stewardship, raising up resources, etc.

- **Willow Creek Resources**®—provides churches with trusted and field-tested ministry resources in such areas as leadership, evangelism, spiritual formation, spiritual gifts, small groups, stewardship, student ministry, children's ministry, the use of the arts-drama, media, contemporary music —and more.

- **WCA Member Benefits**—includes substantial discounts to WCA training events, a 20 percent discount on all Willow Creek Resources®, *Defining Moments* monthly audio journal for leaders, quarterly *Willow* magazine, access to a Members-Only section on WillowNet, monthly communications, and more. Member Churches also receive special discounts and premier services through WCA's growing number of ministry partners—Select Service Providers—and save an average of $500 annually depending on the level of engagement.

For specific information about WCA conferences, resources, membership, and other ministry services contact:

Willow Creek Association
P.O. Box 3188
Barrington, IL 60011-3188
Phone: 847-570-9812
Fax: 847-765-5046
www.willowcreek.com

Continue building your new community!
New Community Series
BILL HYBELS AND JOHN ORTBERG
with Kevin and Sherry Harney

Exodus: *Journey Toward God* 0-310-22771-2

Parables: *Imagine Life God's Way* 0-310-22881-6

Sermon on the Mount¹: *Connect with God* 0-310-22884-0

Sermon on the Mount²: *Connect with Others* 0-310-22883-2

Acts: *Build Community* 0-310-22770-4

Romans: *Find Freedom* 0-310-22765-8

Philippians: *Run the Race* 0-310-22766-6

Colossians: *Discover the New You* 0-310-22769-0

James: *Live Wisely* 0-310-22767-4

1 Peter: *Stand Strong* 0-310-22773-9

1 John: *Love Each Other* 0-310-22768-2

Revelation: *Experience God's Power* 0-310-22882-4

Look for New Community at your local Christian bookstore.

Continue the Transformation
Pursuing Spiritual Transformation
JOHN ORTBERG, LAURIE PEDERSON,
AND JUDSON POLING

Grace: *An Invitation to a Way of Life* 0-310-22074-2

Growth: *Training vs. Trying* 0-310-22075-0

Groups: *The Life-Giving Power of Community* 0-310-22076-9

Gifts: *The Joy of Serving God* 0-310-22077-7

Giving: *Unlocking the Heart of Good Stewardship* 0-310-22078-5

Fully Devoted: *Living Each Day in Jesus' Name* 0-310-22073-4

Look for Pursuing Spiritual Transformation at your local Christian bookstore.

TOUGH QUESTIONS
Garry Poole and Judson Poling

Softcover

How Does Anyone Know God Exists?	ISBN 0-310-24502-8
What Difference Does Jesus Make?	ISBN 0-310-24503-6
How Reliable Is the Bible?	ISBN 0-310-24504-4
How Could God Allow Suffering and Evil?	ISBN 0-310-24505-2
Don't All Religions Lead to God?	ISBN 0-310-24506-0
Do Science and the Bible Conflict?	ISBN 0-310-24507-9
Why Become a Christian?	ISBN 0-310-24508-7
Leader's Guide	ISBN 0-310-24509-5

REALITY CHECK SERIES
by Mark Ashton

Winning at Life	ISBN: 0-310-24525-7
Leadership Jesus Style	ISBN: 0-310-24526-5
When Tragedy Strikes	ISBN: 0-310-24524-9
Sudden Impact	ISBN: 0-310-24522-2
Jesus' Greatest Moments	ISBN: 0-310-24528-1
Hot Issues	ISBN: 0-310-24523-0
Future Shock	ISBN: 0-310-24527-3
Clear Evidence	ISBN: 0-310-24746-2

God Is Closer Than You Think

John Ortberg

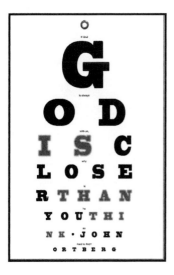

Two works of art help John Ortberg think about the presence of God. One is Michelangelo Buonarroti's brilliant painting of God and Adam on the ceiling of the Sistine Chapel. God is close. His hand comes within a hair's breadth of the hand of the man. It seems to say that God is closer than we think—he's here, now, today, accessible to all who will but "lift a finger."

The second work of art is Martin Hanford's cartoon character Waldo. He is on every page of the Where's Waldo? books, but he can be difficult to find. In the same way, even though God is present on every page of our lives, he's often not easy to spot.

In *God Is Closer Than You Think*, John Ortberg examines this frustrating paradox of the Christian life.

"When it is so easy to 'see' God all around me (in trees, in birds, in nature) why is it so hard to feel his presence—especially when I need him most?"

Ortberg helps readers discover the secret to living daily in the reality of God's most frequent promise in Scripture, "I will be with you."

Hardcover: 0-310-25349-7
ebooks:
Adobe Acrobat eBook Reader® format: 0-310-26336-0
Microsoft Reader® format: 0-310-26337-9
Mobipocket® format: 0-310-26339-5
Palm Reader® format: 0-310-26338-7
Unabridged Audio Pages® CD: 0-310-26379-4
Abridged Audio Pages® CD: 0-310-26450-2

Pick up a copy today at your favorite bookstore!

ZONDERVAN™

GRAND RAPIDS, MICHIGAN 49530 USA
WWW.ZONDERVAN.COM

WILLOW
Willow Creek Association